Band Instrument

"Quick Fix" Repair Solutions

Also available from GIA Publications, Inc.

Band Instrument "Quick Fix" Repair Kit (G-7052)

Including:

- Six-piece screwdriver and awl set with handle
- Small/large spring hook
- Leak light with battery
- Key and rotor oil with pin-hole attachment
- Assortment of eight replacement water key corks

Band Instrument
"Quick Fix" Repair Solutions

Written by a Band Director
for Band Directors

Gregory Biba

GIA Publications, Inc.
Chicago

Band Instrument "Quick Fix" Repair Solutions: Written by a Band Director for Band Directors

Gregory Biba

Cover, layout, and design: Joel A. Sibick

GIA Publications, Inc.
7404 S. Mason Ave., Chicago 60638
Copyright © 2006 GIA Publications, Inc.
Printed in the United States of America

G-6901

ISBN-10: 1-57999-597-7
ISBN-13: 1-978-57999-597-3
www.giamusic.com

To my wife Dawn—
Thanks for everything

Contents

Illustrations

Foreword

The purpose of this book is to introduce both teachers and students to basic maintenance and minor repair techniques associated with the most common problems of different band instruments. Finding the quick fix solution to any repair will save valuable rehearsal or lesson time and could potentially save parents money on repairs, as well as allowing the band director to use budget money on only necessary repairs.

Repairs typically sent to a repair shop are often simple and could instead be handled easily by the band director or a student.

Sometimes repair and maintenance manuals are too technical and complicated. More condensed, simplified instructions will help lead directors or students through repairs in a step-by-step process. Remember, any time you attempt a repair, to make sure the instrument's condition will be improved, not worsened.

When directors show students how to handle their own minor or emergency repairs, it will enable the young musicians to learn how to care for their own instruments.

The recommended repair tools can be obtained from any qualified repair technician; a basic kit is available from GIA Publications.

—Greg Biba

UNIT 1

BRASS INSTRUMENTS

Chapter 1
General Care

To keep brass instruments out of the repair shop, students need to be reminded that cleaning certain parts of the instrument on a regular basis is essential. Damaging moisture comes in the form of condensation created when warm air meets cold brass. Saliva comes in much smaller amounts. The metal becomes corroded from the resulting oxidation reaction. The lead-pipe is a common area where small pink spots appear outside the tubing. These red spots, called red rot, develop from the process of the copper and nickel in the brass separating through corrosion. Always remind students to remove the mouthpiece from the instrument when it is not being played. Also encourage students to clean both the mouthpiece and lead-pipe with lukewarm water and a mild liquid soap (Dawn, ERA, etc.). Each student should have a schedule of cleaning and oiling valves, slides, springs, and mouthpiece.

Minimum Essential Tools and Accessories
for the Repair and Maintenance
of Brass Instruments

Tools

Mouthpiece puller
Mouthpiece brushes
Rawhide mallet
Pliers (needle-nose and round-nose)
Screwdrivers (assorted sizes/large and small)
Mouthpiece truer
Scissors
Thin leather belt

Accessories

Penetrating oil (Ferree's Tools, Inc., catalog
   #J88/Corrosion Cracker)
WD-40
Valentino water key corks (assorted sizes)
Trumpet mouthpiece Jam Stopper (G & D
   Enterprises)
Cork valve washers
Felt valve washers

NEVER USE SUPER GLUE.

NEVER USE RUBBER BANDS ON METAL;
CORROSION WILL OCCUR.

for the Repair and Maintenance of Brass Instruments

Piston Valve Instruments: Trumpet/Cornet, Euphonium/Baritone, Tuba	Slide Instrument: Trombone	Rotary Valve Instrument: French Horn

Piston Valve Instruments

Tools

Valve brush

Accessories

Valve oil

   Three sets of bottom valve springs (one for each: trumpet, cornet, euphonium/baritone, tuba)

Assorted valve stem felts for the above instruments

Valentino water key corks for the above instruments

Trumpet mouthpiece Jam Stopper (G & D Enterprises)

Toothpaste

Slide Instrument: Trombone

Tools

Trombone snake or brush

Accessories

Slide oil

Valentino water key corks

Trombone Slide Bow Protector (DEG Music) —prevents crook from getting smashed

Rotary Valve Instrument: French Horn

Tools

Screwdriver with thin-tipped blade

Accessories

Rotary valve oil

Several feet of braided, 30-pound test fishing line

Stuck Mouthpiece

If directors had a nickel for every time they had to remove a stuck mouthpiece, it would be easy to become a millionaire. This is most frustrating when a student's mouthpiece becomes stuck on the instrument at home and someone decides to remove it by putting the mouthpiece receiver/lead-pipe in a vise and twisting and pulling on it with pliers. This may require taking the instrument to the repair shop to solder a broken brace, in addition to other possible repairs.

At the first lesson it is crucial to tell students to always remove the mouthpiece when putting the horn away because the action of salivary acids will cause the mouthpiece to become stuck. Even though the "popping" sound caused by giving the mouthpiece a whack is fun to listen to, this will force the mouthpiece into the horn beyond its normal placement. A gentle clockwise twist into mouthpiece receiver is sufficient to tighten it. Even with these reminders, the instrument may accidentally be dropped. Some procedures to remove the mouthpiece follow.

Materials Needed:

1. Small rawhide mallet
2. Mouthpiece puller for all brass instruments (Bobcat or Thompson)
3. Trumpet mouthpiece Jam Stopper (G & D Enterprises)

Stuck Mouthpiece

Procedure:

1. Make sure to support the braces and tubing as you grasp the instrument securely under one arm.
2. With one hand, pull on the mouthpiece and twist; with the other hand, tap the mouthpiece receiver with a rawhide mallet. Grinding one end of a rawhide mallet to a "V" helps you to more accurately hit the right point for freeing mouthpieces. (See Figure 1.1, Figure 1.2, and Figure 1.3.)

Figure 1.1. Removing Stuck Mouthpiece by Tapping on Receiver (Trumpet)

Figure 1.2. Removing Stuck Mouthpiece by Tapping on Receiver (French Horn)

Figure 1.3. Removing Stuck Mouthpiece by Tapping on Receiver (Trombone)

Words of wisdom: When working with the trombone—
1. Be certain to lock the slide.
2. Strike on the mouthpiece receiver, NOT the cork barrel.

Stuck Mouthpiece

Over the years, my favorite mouthpiece puller has been the Bobcat (Figure 1.4). (Thompson pullers also work well, as do some pistol-grip pullers.)

To use this tool, simply place the bottom two jaws of the puller against the receiver and secure them by tightening both nuts on the underside of each jaw. By unscrewing the long threaded bolts evenly, the top portion of the puller will push up against the cup of the mouthpiece.

Figure 1.4. Bobcat Mouthpiece Puller

Words of wisdom: Hold the lead-pipe brace so that if the brace became loose when the mouthpiece got jammed it will not break during the twisting of the adjustment screws. Please do not force the adjustment screws too hard, or the lead-pipe brace will break.

Stuck Mouthpiece

Another preventative maintenance product that can be used with accident-prone trumpet players is the trumpet mouthpiece Jam Stopper (Figure 1.5).

Once adjusted onto the mouthpiece shank, this ingenious accessory prevents the mouthpiece from ever getting stuck. One end of the Jam Stopper rests against the mouthpiece receiver, and the other end unscrews to meet against the cup portion of the mouthpiece.

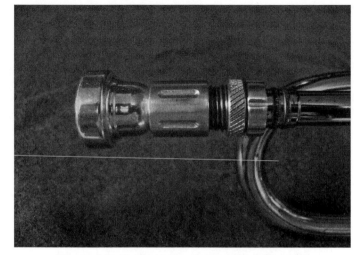

Figure 1.5. Trumpet Mouthpiece Jam Stopper

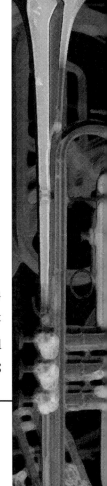

Cleaning the Mouthpiece

Supplying the students with mouthpiece brushes is essential for keeping the mouthpiece from becoming filled with "mold". If the mold inside the mouthpiece is thick and hard, it can be softened and removed by soaking it in vinegar for half an hour or longer. Remind students to use warm, soapy water to keep the mouthpiece clean.

Straightening the Mouthpiece

Mouthpieces can get stuck due to the shank of the mouthpiece being bent. Use a mouthpiece truer and possibly a rawhide mallet to help round the end (Figure 1.6).

Procedure:

1. Hold the mouthpiece firmly in your hand.
2. Insert the pointed end of the mouthpiece truer in the open shank of the mouthpiece.
3. Only insert the truer as far as needed to make the end of the mouthpiece (shank) round. (Be careful not to split the end of the shank.)
4. The open (shank) end of the mouthpiece usually is made of thin metal. Roll the tip of the truer around to make the end of the mouthpiece round.

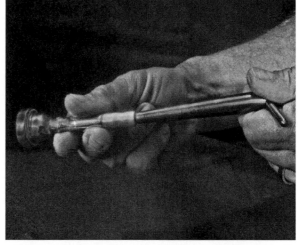

Figure 1.6. Straightening the Bent (Shank) End of the Mouthpiece with a Mouthpiece Truer

You can clean the mouthpiece shank with a "scrubby" pad (nonabrasive) to prevent it from getting stuck again.

11

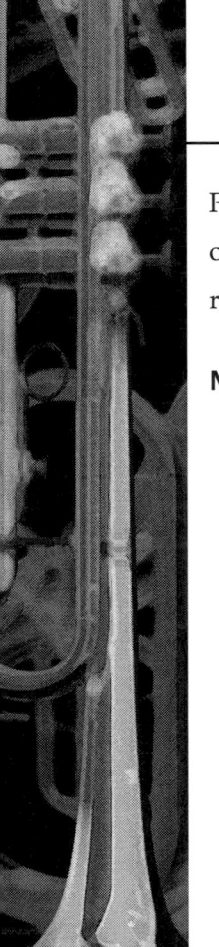

Stuck Tuning Slides

Piston- and rotary-valve instrument slides will become stuck if not properly lubricated. Trumpet players often neglect lubricating the first- and second-valve slides. The following procedure explains how to remove a stuck slide.

Materials Needed:

1. Cloth (handkerchief)
2. Rawhide mallet
3. Penetrating oil
4. Drumstick
5. Slide lubricant
6. Brass polish (Brasso) or 0000 steel wool
7. Valentino pad assortments

Stuck Tuning Slides

Procedure (Removing, Cleaning, and Replacing):

1. Hold the instrument firmly under your arm and close to your body.

2. Wrap a cloth handkerchief around the stuck slide (Figures 1.7 and 1.8).

3. While holding the instrument firmly, or better yet, having someone else hold the instrument, give a series of even, straight jerks to the cloth handkerchief. Do not jerk too hard as you can kink or collapse the slide and instrument. (Repetition is more important than the power used.)

Figure 1.7. Removing Stuck Tuning Slide
(Trumpet)

Figure 1.8. Removing Stuck Tuning Slide
(French Horn)

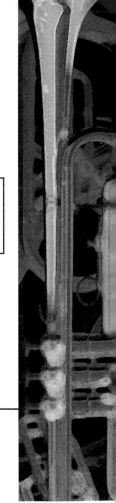

Stuck Tuning Slides

4. If the slide is still frozen, gently tap on the outer part of the slide using a rawhide mallet to loosen up any corrosion. Use in conjunction with penetrating oil. Be careful because dents can occur easily. A qualified repair technician can take care of frozen slides if gentle taps do not loosen corrosion.

Words of wisdom: If a tuning slide on a French horn is stuck, use the ball end of a snare drum stick. Place the ball end behind the slide brace, and gently tap nearest to the ball end of the stick with a rawhide mallet.

Stuck Tuning Slides

5. When trying to remove or replace the trombone tuning slide, use even pressure so the slide does not become cocked or stuck. In removing the trombone tuning slide, grasp the outer portion of the trombone at the bell brace (Figure 1.9). Push up with your thumbs against the balancer.

In replacing the trombone tuning slide, the thumbs should be hooked under the bell brace (Figure 1.10) and fingers placed over the top of the balancer to evenly push the slide in.

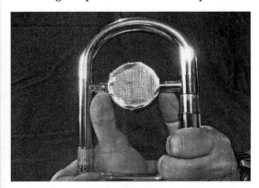

Figure 1.9. Removing Tuning Slide
(Trombone)

Figure 1.10. Replacing Tuning Slide
(Trombone)

Stuck Tuning Slides

Do not rock the tuning slide back and forth! If the slide becomes cocked because it was not evenly pushed or pulled out, gently tap on the low side of the balancer with a rawhide mallet.

6. If the slide remains frozen, apply some penetrating oil to the tubing, and let it stand overnight before trying to remove the stuck slide again. After applying penetrating oil, the instrument needs to be flushed and cleaned, as most penetrating oils are toxic and leave a bad taste. Professionals use Ferree's Corrosion Cracker (Feree's Tools, Inc., catalog #J88—the two ounce bottle with bench oil attachment is typical).

7. When the slide is finally removed, clean the corrosion off by soaking the slide in vinegar for thirty minutes before wiping it off with some water. To remove excess corrosion, gently wipe the slide off with 0000 steel wool or fine emery paper (600 grit). Use slide lubricant to completely clean it off.

Stuck Tuning Slides

8. To make sure that both ends of the tuning slide will go in evenly, use tuning-slide lubricant on both male ends. Each lubricated end of the tuning slide should be pushed into the open female ends of the trombone one at a time to ensure even distribution of the cream (Figure 1.11).

Do not push the tuning slide on while the instrument is resting on the floor. That pressure could damage the hand slide. Instead, balance the bell on your knee or remove the hand slide before doing tuning slide work.

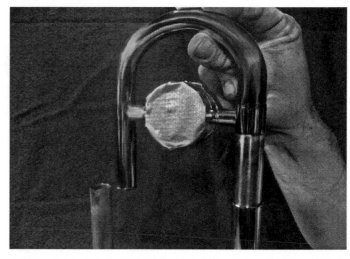

Figure 1.11. Re-greasing/Replacing Tuning Slide (Trombone)

17

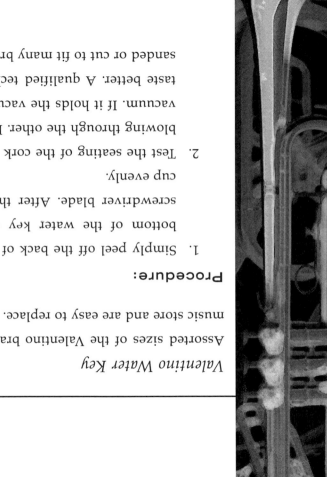

Valentino Water Key

Assorted sizes of the Valentino brand water key (spit valve) corks can be purchased from your local music store and are easy to replace.

Procedure:

1. Simply peel off the back of the cork to expose the sticky portion, which will be placed in the bottom of the water key cup. Make sure you have scraped out the excess crud with a screwdriver blade. After the key cup is clean and dry, place the pad in the bottom of the cup evenly.

2. Test the seating of the cork by placing the thumb over the end of one tube of the slide and by blowing through the other. If it leaks, shift the cork and test again. Or try sucking in to create a vacuum. If it holds the vacuum, then it does not leak. Blowing out is not as accurate, but does taste better. A qualified technician can install regular cork, and it can be pressure fitted and sanded or cut to fit to many brands.

Water Keys

Amado Water Key

To keep the water key from getting stuck, put a drop of valve oil in the middle hole to lubricate. If the water key pin gets stuck, unfold a paper clip and push the pin back out by inserting the paper clip through the hole, and then oil the outside of the water key pin to lubricate (Figure 1.12).

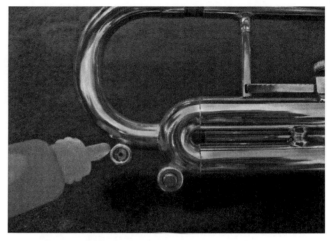

Figure 1.12. Oiling Amado Water Key (Trumpet)

NEVER PUSH THE PIN
IN WITH PENCIL LEAD.

Chapter 2
Piston Valve Instruments
Trumpet/Cornet, Euphonium/Baritone, Tuba
Cleaning and Lubrication

Valves and slides should be removed and the inside of the entire instrument washed and flushed on a regular basis. Once per month keeps most brass instruments clean inside.

Students should exercise great care when brushing and flushing because valves and slides could be damaged by banging them against the sink when removed.

Materials Needed:

1. Flexible brush

2. Valve oil

3. Specially formulated tuning slide grease

4. Clean rags or towels

5. Mild liquid soap (Dawn or ERA, with a degreasing agent)

6. Valve casing cleaning rod

Cleaning and Lubrication

Procedure (Disassembling and Cleaning):

1. Have a sink or bathtub of warm (not hot!), sudsy water.
2. Keep the valves in order as you remove them and wipe them off with a clean cloth.
3. Wipe off springs; it is important to keep them with the valves. Make sure that when the springs are removed, they go back in the same valve casing.
4. Wipe off the bottom valve caps.
5. Pull all the slides and wipe off the old grease.
6. Submerge the body of the instrument in the warm water for about ten minutes.
7. Use the slide brush and clean out sides while underwater. Pour the liquid soap directly on the brushes for best cleaning. Remember to wipe them dry.
8. Empty the horn of all water by turning it over several times to get the water out of all the crooks.
9. Dry off the horn.
10. Wipe out the bathtub after cleaning to prevent a greasy ring from forming on the sides of the tub.

Cleaning and Lubrication

Procedure (Greasing, Oiling, and Assembling):

1. Use a valve brush, not a rod, to clean the valve casing. Dip the brush directly into the soap and scrub.

2. Gently insert the brush into the valve casing and twist to remove extra grime or water.

3. To clean the outside of the valve, use liquid soap (Dawn or ERA) and make sure to wipe clean.

4. Take the bottom and top valve caps and put Vaseline or slide grease on the threads before replacing.

5. The springs can also be given a thin coating of petroleum jelly before replacing.

6. When cleaning valves, be careful not to get the valve felts wet.

7. Before putting the valves back, put several drops of valve oil on each. I suggest the brand Blue Juice.

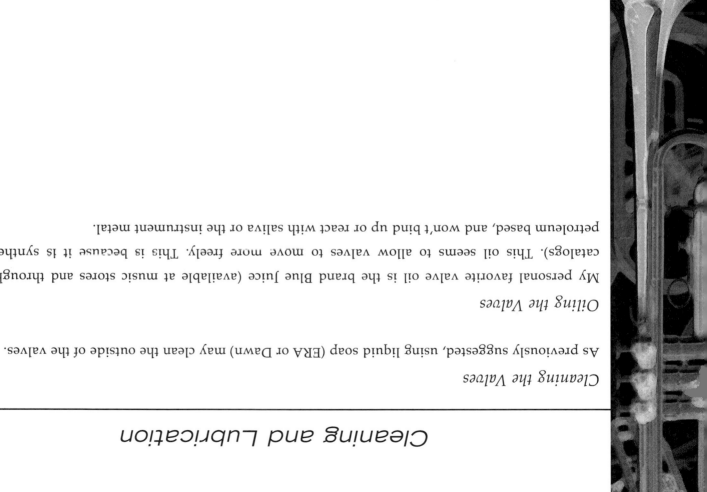

Cleaning and Lubrication

Cleaning the Valves

As previously suggested, using liquid soap (ERA or Dawn) may clean the outside of the valves.

Oiling the Valves

My personal favorite valve oil is the brand **Blue Juice** (available at music stores and through music catalogs). This oil seems to allow valves to move more freely. This is because it is synthetic, not petroleum based, and won't bind up or react with saliva or the instrument metal.

Valve Caps

Over the years, students have come to school many times with a stuck valve cap. In addition, the threads of the cap are often stripped because someone at home used pliers with no protective covering over the threads to try to loosen it. The following steps should be used to loosen the stuck valve cap.

Materials Needed:

1. Pliers
2. Rawhide mallet
3. Piece of leather belt
4. Tuning-slide grease

Figure 2.1. Removing Stuck Valve Cap (Trumpet)

Procedure:

1. Try tapping around the rim of the cap with a rawhide mallet to loosen the corrosion. Gently tapping on the top may also help.
2. If this fails, try applying penetrating oil and let sit overnight. Then tap gently.
3. Remove as many valve caps as possible.
4. Place the leather belt around the stuck cap.
5. Twist to unscrew (Figure 2.1).
6. Clean the inside of the cap and the threads. Use tuning-slide grease on the threads before replacing.

Placement of the Valve Guides

Look for the numbers located on each valve, and always put them back in the correct valve casing. The first valve is nearest to the mouthpiece, and the third valve is nearest to the bell.

Valve Damage

When a valve is not going up and down smoothly, check to see if it is the valve or the valve casing. After removing the valve, try putting it in another valve casing to see if it goes up and down smoothly. If it goes up and down smoothly, the valve casing is probably very dirty and needs cleaning. If the valve gets stuck in another valve casing, then the problem is with the valve, and you should have a qualified repair technician check out the valve problem.

If the second valve is not going up and down, the second-valve tuning slide could have a small dent. When the second-valve tuning slide was dented, it probably forced the second-valve casing to be out of alignment. Before the repair technician inspects the second valve or the second-valve casing problem, try bending the second-valve tuning slide out and away (toward the third-valve casing) to see if it allows the second valve to move up and down smoothly.

The Valves

If a valve has not been oiled for an extended period of time, it will probably be stuck within the valve casing. To remove the stuck valve, perform the following steps:

1. Tap gently on the finger button with a rawhide mallet (very gently). On newer horns, do not tap on finger buttons because they have plastic perils that will crack. Use the palm of your hand.

Figure 2.2. Placement of Valve Guides, "Click" Valves in Place (Trumpet)

Words of wisdom: Listen for a clicking sound as the finger button is slowly turned clockwise. Note that the numbers on the individual valves on the different brands of trumpet should all be either facing toward you or away from you. Look at the side view (Figure 2.2).

2. In an emergency only, remove the bottom valve cap and watch for any springs that could fall out.

3. Professional technicians suggest using another valve going up from the bottom. As a last resort, take a cushioned dowel or drumstick, and position it against the bottom of the valve (Figure 2.3).

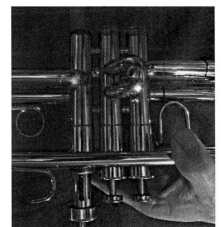

Figure 2.3. Removing Stuck Valve with the Use of Another Valve up from the Bottom (Trumpet)

As a last resort, remove stuck valve with a cushioned drumstick or dowel.

Valve-slide flexing should only be done with the valve in the casing.

The Valves

4. When using a cushioned dowel or drumstick as a last resort, tap the end of the dowel or drumstick gently with a rawhide mallet.

5. Use some tuning-slide grease on the bottom valve cap, and then oil the valve before putting it back into the valve casing. If the valve does not move up and down smoothly, there was probably some previous damage, and a certified instrument repair technician should be contacted.

Valve Buttons

If an instrument makes a clicking sound as the valve is depressed, try tightening the valve cap.

Have an assortment of corks and felts on hand to replace those wearing out. Make sure to replace the worn out cork or felt exactly as you would the valves that are working properly.

Valve Adjustment Cork and Felts

Make sure to check that the height of the three valves is the same after replacing worn corks or felts.

The Valves

On some horns there is a mark on the valve stem that should be even with the top of the valve cap. If this is uneven and you notice the three valves are not at the same level, try the following.

(Replace all three porting felts at the same time, never only one.)

1. Add a cork shim to the top of the existing cork. This lies on top of the valve.
2. Cut off about 1/16 inch from a tube of cork, or use precut cork shims.
3. The cork shim will be under a precut piece of felt and placed over the top of the valve stem.

Valve Springs

Remind students to be careful when they unscrew the bottom valve cap. The valve spring could fall out. (Have an assortment of springs on hand for the various brass instruments.)

Water-Key Springs

If the cork in the water key (spit valve) leaks, check the tension of the water-key spring.

Materials Needed:

1. Needle-nosed pliers

Procedure:

1. Hold the spring tightly in the pliers.
2. Pull and bend the spring back and down.
3. Be careful not to bend the spring too much, or it will break.

Additional Troubleshooting Options

Euphonium – Yamaha/Jupiter Brand
(Exposed Valve Breather Hole)

When there is no sound and the valves click into place, try the following:

1. Check the white caps that are under the valve stems.
2. Recognize that the cap has one peg on the underside (Figure 2.4).
3. Take off the finger button.
4. Take the valve cap off.
5. Look to see if the peg that is on the underside of the white cap is positioned in the small guide hole on top of the valve.

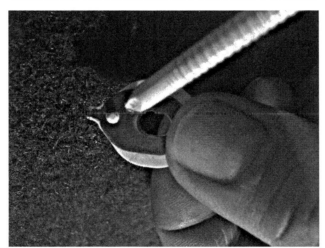

Figure 2.4. White Cap with Peg Inserts into Small Guide Pin Hole on Top of Valve (Euphonium)

6. Remember that half of the large breather hole is exposed (Figure 2.5).

7. Tighten the valve stem (if needed).

8. Put valve cap back on over the valve stem and screw on the finger button.

9. Reoil the valve if needed.

10. Click the valve back in place.

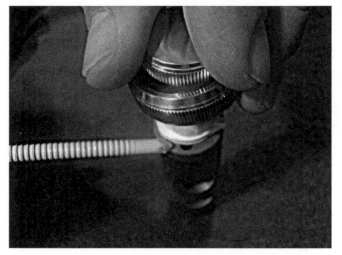

Figure 2.5. Top of Valve Breather Hole Is Exposed
(Euphonium)

Additional Troubleshooting Options

Trumpet (Enclosed Valve Guides)

If the valve does not respond properly and there is no visible damage, the guide may be upside down. Take the piston apart, turn the guide over, and reassemble (Figure 2.6).

The white plastic guide that rests under the spring should be turned over to match the other valve guides if needed.

Trumpet (Stuffy Low D)

If the low D sounds stuffy, check to see if the water-key cork (spit valve) is sealing over the hole. If the water-key cork itself is not worn, check to see if the screw that holds the water-key cork on needs to be retightened.

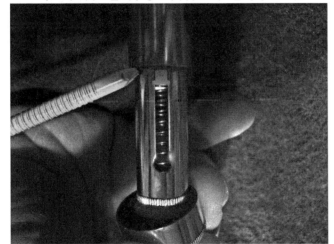

Figure 2.6. Enclosed Valve Guide Troubleshooting (Trumpet)

Slide Instrument
Trombone
Cleaning and Lubrication

Remind students that it is their responsibility to make sure the slide is clean and lubricated. The process for cleaning a trombone follows.

Materials Needed:

1. Slide oil

2. Valve oil

3. Trombone cleaning snake

4. Mild detergent soap

Procedure (Disassembling and Cleaning):

1. Fill a large sink or bathtub with lukewarm, sudsy water.

2. Disassemble the tuning slide from the bell.

3. Submerge the tuning slide and bell into the water.

4. Use the flexible snake to clean out dirt and grime.

5. Rinse in clear water to remove soap scum and wipe out all parts.

6. Now do the same for the inner and outer hand slides.

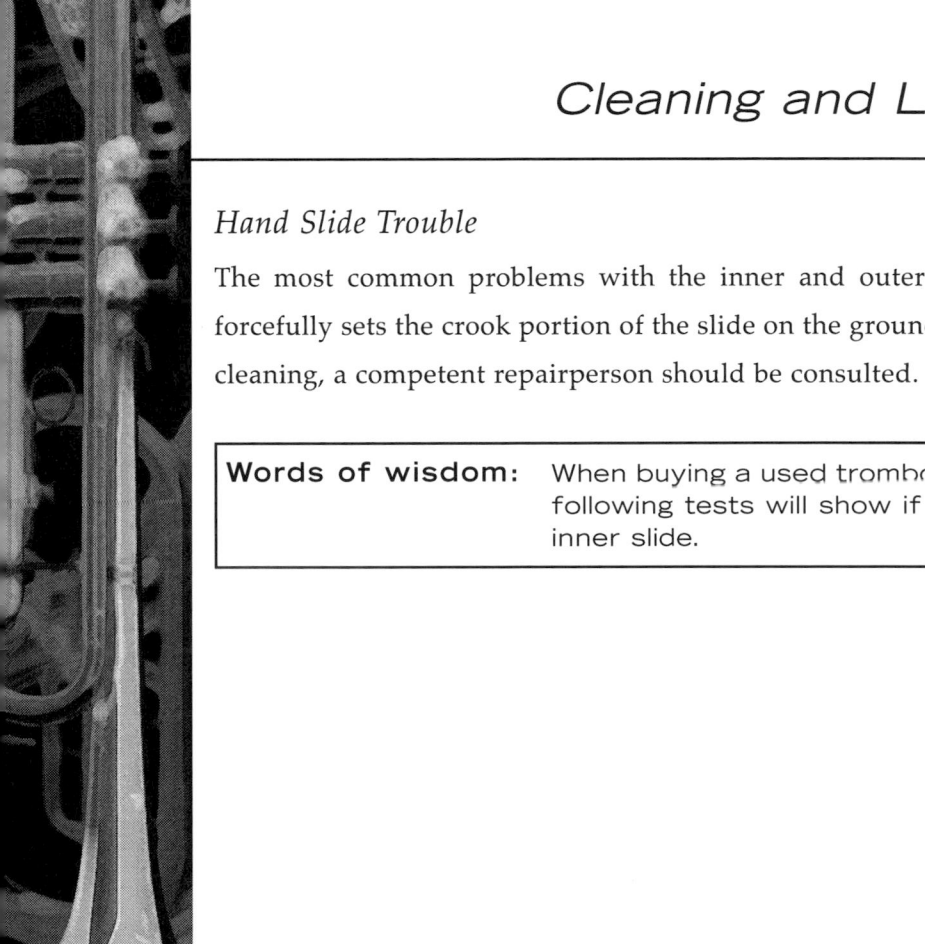

Cleaning and Lubrication

Hand Slide Trouble

The most common problems with the inner and outer portion of the slide occur when a musician forcefully sets the crook portion of the slide on the ground when not playing. If the slide still drags after cleaning, a competent repairperson should be consulted.

Words of wisdom:	When buying a used trombone, check the condition of the slide. The following tests will show if there has been any excess wear to the inner slide.

Cleaning and Lubrication

Procedure 1 (Preferred Method):

Balance the hand slide on the ground and lift up on the inner slide. If the outer slide remains on the floor without jerking up, the action is smooth. If it sticks, you can tell where the problem is and have a certified repair technician fix it.

Procedure 2:

Set the assembled slide on the floor, and pull the inner slide about halfway up and out. Close off one of the tubes of the inner slide with the hand; with the mouth, suck in on the outer tubing. If the slide is in good condition, the suction created should raise the outer slide up and off the floor. (See *Practical Band Instrument Repair Manual* by Clayton H. Tiede, p. 29.)

Smashed Crook

As previously mentioned, remind students that the bow area of the slide is one of the areas where much damage occurs. These problems usually occur when the musician forcefully rests the bow on the ground when not playing.

To prevent the bow (crook) portion of the slide from being smashed in, I recommend purchasing the Trombone Slide Bow Protector (DEG Music) (Figure 3.1). This cover simply snaps onto the outer portion of the crook. The musician still has access to the water key (Figure 3.2).

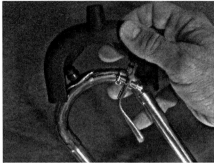

Figure 3.2. Trombone Slide Bow Protector – Snaps onto Crook

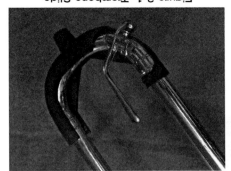

Figure 3.1. Trombone Slide Bow Protector

When there is a broken valve string, which is a very common problem, it is often because a valve is stuck and the musician forcibly depresses the valve key.

Oiling the valves should be done at least every few weeks. This can be done by removing the valve cap and oiling the exposed shaft as it is rotated (Figure 4.1).

Figure 4.1. Oiling Exposed Shaft (French Horn)

Oiling the Valves (Temporary)

To oil the top bearing, the following procedure should be used:

Procedure:

1. Loosen the stop arm head screw about three turns.

2. Lift the stop arm head enough so the oil can run in on top of the bearing surface (Figure 4.2).

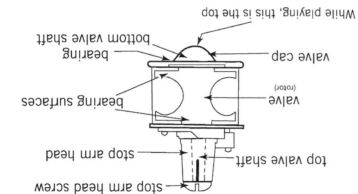

stop arm head screw

stop arm head

top valve shaft

bearing surfaces

valve
(rotor)

bearing
bottom valve shaft

valve cap

While playing, this is the top

Figure 4.2. Oiling Top Bearing (French Horn)

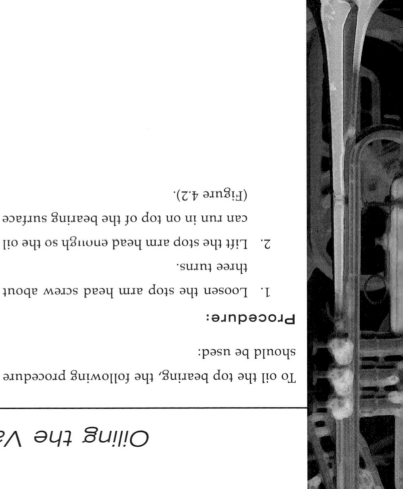

Valve action can be greatly improved if the levers are as close to the stop arm as possible (Figure 4.3). (Being parallel to the rotor shaft is very important.)

Lever A is in the correct position for effective stringing. Reminder: never adjust the height of the three keys by bending the key paddles.

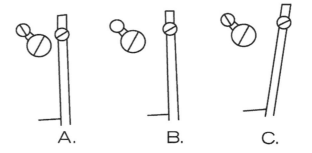

A. B. C.

Rotary Valve
Inst
French Horn

Figure 4.3. Lever Arm Positioning (French Horn)

Valve Restringing

The string used should be woven rayon or nylon and of 30–50-pound test fishing line. Tie the string as shown, with the string wrapping under itself to lock it under the screws (Figure 4.4). When stringing, tighten the stop arm screw lightly to hold the lever while you finish stringing.

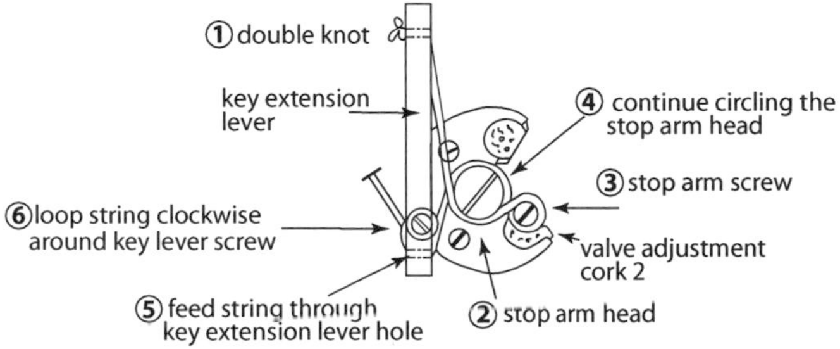

Procedure:

1. Loosen both the stop arm screw and the key lever screw and remove the broken string.
2. Cut a piece of string to seven or eight inches.
3. Tie a double knot in one end.

Figure 4.4. Proper Restringing (French Horn)

① double knot
② stop arm head
③ stop arm screw
④ continue circling the stop arm head
⑤ feed string through key extension lever hole
⑥ loop string clockwise around key lever screw

valve adjustment cork 2
key extension lever

Valve Restringing

4. Feed the string through the hole of the key extension lever with the knot on the opposite side from the valve.

5. Run the string around behind the stop arm head, twist a loop in the string, and slip it over the top of the stop arm screw. Note the direction of the string and the correct overlapping. Do not tighten this screw yet. Continue circling the stop arm head with the string, and feed it through the hole in the end of the key extension lever.

6. Loop the string around the key lever screw in a clockwise direction, pull it tight, and tighten the screw.

7. Check and adjust the height of the valve key lever. As the stop arm screw is held against the valve adjustment cork #2, move the valve key lever to a level height compared to the other valve key levers.

8. Hold the key lever in this level position and tighten the stop arm screw.

Rotary Valve
Inst
French Horn

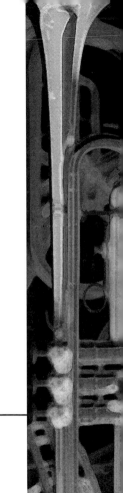

Additional Troubleshooting Options

Problem: Valve (rotor) sticking

Solution: Loosen valve cap slightly or loosen the key lever screw a very small amount. Another option is to tap the stop arm head screw gently with a rawhide mallet. This screw is located on top of the valve shaft (valve stem). This will break the seal caused by saliva containing sugar that has dried and secured the valve, and the valve should move.

Figure 4.5. Removing Stuck Tuning Slide
(French Horn)

Problem: Stuck tuning slide

Solution: If a tuning slide on a French horn is stuck, use the ball end of a snare drum stick. Place the ball end behind the slide brace, and gently tap as close to the ball end of the stick as possible with a rawhide mallet (Figure 4.5).

UNIT 2

WOODWIND INSTRUMENTS

Chapter 5
General Care

One of the most important reminders for any woodwind player is to get rid of as much excess moisture from the instrument as possible.

Moisture appears in the form of condensation from the breath and saliva in the mouth. When water is absorbed into a wooden instrument, the body swells and shrinks unevenly because the inside dries out more slowly than the outside. One of the reasons wood cracks is because the natural oils evaporate around the tone holes and in the bore. Sudden temperature changes also put stress on the wood.

If wood becomes too dry, it will pull away from the metal key posts, causing them to become loose. If one of these posts is supporting a needle spring, the tension from the spring can cause the post to turn, thus binding the keys. (Tenon rings can also become loose when wood dries out and retracts.) Some other reasons students should always swab out all sections of the instrument and avoid any exposure to sudden temperature changes are to keep the bore of the instrument clean and to draw moisture away from the pads, which extends the life of the pad and prevents residue buildup. Also, when tone holes change shape, joints shrink and don't fit, steel rods rust, and keys become bound.

Minimum Essential Tools and Accessories for the Repair and Maintenance of Woodwind Instruments

Tools

Needle-nose pliers
Screwdrivers (assorted sizes/large and small)
Mouthpiece brushes
Razor blade
Feeler gauge
Spring hook
Tweezers

Accessories

Valentino replacement cork
Valentino replacement pads (peel-off backing)
Bore oil
Pad and cork cement
Cork grease
Contact cement
Felt bumpers
Prick punch—needle (used to poke small hole in edge of bladder pad to relieve trapped air or moisture and for installation of new pad)
Emery board (used to smooth out excess tenon cork, especially when new)

Cleaning the Pads

Pads eventually absorb spit, sugar, food, moisture from the body, and dust and foreign matter, resulting in a sticky pad. To clean the pads:

1. Place a crisp, new dollar bill that is not dirty (for leather pads) or a piece of cigarette paper (for skin pads) between the pad and the tone hole.
2. Press the pad down and withdraw. (It could take several times to get rid of the sticky sound.)

Woodwind
General
Care

Cleaning the Body

Acids are formed in the mouth in varying amounts depending on what is consumed (sugar from soda, food, etc.). These acids are a problem for metal woodwinds. Remind students to rinse their mouths with water prior to playing to lessen the acid concentration of the saliva.

Swabbing out all of the parts of a woodwind instrument is crucial to preventing poor intonation and to having a good tone. Dirt or other food particles will cause the throat tones of a clarinet to speak poorly and prevent an oboe or saxophone from overblowing its octave properly. Also, when swabbing out the individual parts of the clarinet, dry off the inside ledges of the barrel and the inside ledge of the lower tenon joint because water collects there.

Repairs and Maintenance on the Body

Cracks

Cracks that are noticed in grenadilla wood clarinets should be taken to a professional repairperson. Prior to taking the instrument to the repair shop, mark the crack with tape or a pencil mark because the wood may swell and close the cracks. The preferred method of closing the crack is called "pinning."

Loose Tenon Rings

When a wooden clarinet dries out, the wood shrinks. This process results in the tenon rings, metal bands that fit around the rim of the tenon receiver, becoming loose.

The emergency procedure to replace a loose tenon ring with a cloth shim is as follows:

Materials Needed:

1. Small square of thin cloth (handkerchief)
2. Razor blade
3. Small rawhide mallet
4. Tube of liquid pad cement

Repairs and Maintenance on the Body

Procedure:

1. Remove the loose ring with a twisting motion, or pry it off with a knife. Make sure to replace the ring the same way you took it off because it is slightly beveled.

2. Clean the inside of the ring that was taken off and the ring inset, which is where you took the ring off (Figure 5.1). (The tenon ring pictured in Figure 5.1 is from an older brand of clarinet and includes a lyre holder feature on the ring.)

3. Spread a thin coat of pad cement on the ring inset.

Figure 5.1 Loose Ring Taken Off Ring Inset
(Clarinet)

4. Stretch the thin cloth evenly over the end (Figure 5.2).

5. Use a rawhide mallet to finish driving the ring evenly over the ring inset (leave about 1/32 inch from the inset shoulder). Use gentle taps only.

6. With a razor blade, cut off the cloth between the ring and the inset shoulder (Figure 5.3).

7. Gently tap the ring all the way down. If the ring is forced on, the cloth is too thick and it will distort the inside of the receiver.

Figure 5.2. Thin Cloth Stretched over
End (Clarinet)

Figure 5.3. Cutting Off Excess Cloth
below Ring (Clarinet)

8. Cut away the cloth that covers the hole (Figure 5.4).

Tenon Recorking – Emergency

1. Valentino cork: Have an assortment of sizes of replacement Valentino cork for all clarinets and saxophones. Peel the back off, and stick on where needed.

2. Recoating cork with cork grease and flame: After greasing the tenon with cork grease, rotate the tenon over a small flame. Keep the tenon rotating so it does not burn. The grease and heat combination will cause the cork to swell. Be very careful—wood burns, and plastic melts even easier.

3. Dental floss: If needed, floss can be used to replace the entire lost tenon cork. Floss has a texture and coating that will compress itself and form a smooth, compact surface. Teflon tape over the tenon cork could be used as well.

Figure 5.4. Cutting Away Inner Cloth inside Ring (Clarinet)

Repairs and Maintenance on the Mechanism

Springs

Improper key action or keys that move sluggishly are probably the result of a bent key, bent hinge rod, bent hinge tube, or bent or twisted posts. A bad spring results in a key that flops or bounces. Start by unhooking the needle spring. If the key moves freely, then continue. If the key is sticky or sluggish, send the instrument in to be repaired by a competent repairman. By using a spring hook, push the weakened needle spring in the opposite direction slightly. This will give the additional tension needed to make the key more responsive. Additional spring replacement work should be done by a competent repairperson.

Key Recorking

Valentino cork is taken from a large sheet for various replacement areas to eliminate lost or excess motion and to eliminate noise. Valentino cork is precut to size.

Pads

Valentino pads can be used to replace worn or missing pads until a pad made of fish skin and felt, leather, or cork is available.

Repairs and Maintenance on the Mechanism

Pad Replacing – Bladder Type

When replacing a bladder pad, take a needle and poke a hole in the edge of the pad to allow air to escape so it will seat better. Put a small amount of cement in the center of the underside of the pad. Some technicians like to heat the key cup just prior to inserting the pad, allowing for a more level and tight-fitting pad. Bring the key down with no real pressure. Valentino replacement pads are also excellent and can hold for months.

Pad Seating

Let the cup cool until the cement has hardened. Then hold the key closed and apply pressure against the cup to seat the pad. Insert the tip of the feeler gauge between the pad and the rim of the tone hole. Depress the key lightly, pull the feeler gauge out slowly, and test for drag. The drag should be noticeable and of the same amount wherever you pull out the feeler gauge.

Additional Troubleshooting Options

Problem: Stuck swab

Solution: When there is a stuck swab, remember to work the swab backwards. Pulling a swab through will make it jam even more. Use a long tool such as a wooden dowel. (Be careful not to scratch the inside of the instrument.) Twist the swab onto the long dowel or button hook tool, and work it backwards.

Problem: Missing hinge rod/pivot screws (emergency)

Solution: Use bent paper clips to hold the rod in place, or use fishing line in the screw hole and tie the guard in place.

Problem: Loose pad (emergency)

Solution: Use a small amount of chewing gum to act as pad cement.

Additional Troubleshooting Options

Problem: Loose screw (emergency)

Solution: Put a drop of clear nail polish on the screw head to hold it in place. Even taking a strand of hair and wrapping it around the threads will help temporarily.

Problem: Tenon cork too loose (emergency)

Solution: Wrap masking tape over the cork, grease the tape, and assemble. Other options include wrapping dental floss around the loose tenon or using Valentino cork sized to fit.

Bridge Mechanism

The bridge keys go out of adjustment more than any other keys. If they are bent, straighten them slowly and carefully, and recork the bottom of the upper bridge if needed (Figure 6.1). (Cut a piece of Valentino replacement cork and size to fit.) Use needle-nose pliers that have smooth jaws, or bend keys by hand.

If the clarinet fails to sound as the clarinetist plays notes below low E (bottom of the staff), it could be due to the fact that the left hand middle finger is not closing enough.

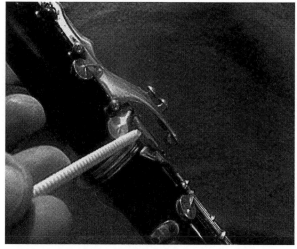

Figure 6.1. Adjust Bottom of Upper Bridge Key (Clarinet)

Woodwind
Clarinet

59

Common Adjustment Problems

The D key that is depressed by the left-hand middle finger will feel spongy (Figure 6.2).

When the bridge key needs adjustments, the pad above the left-hand middle finger does not close far enough (Figure 6.3).

Figure 6.2. Left-Hand Middle Finger "D" Feels Spongy (Clarinet)

Figure 6.3. Pad Above Left-Hand Middle Finger Not Closing Enough (Clarinet)

If the pad above the left-hand middle finger is not seating, bend the upper bridge key down. This can be done by hand as well (Figure 6.4). A feeler gauge and leak light are helpful for checking whether pads are seating properly.

If the low B-flat key (first finger right hand) is not seating, bend the upper bridge key up. This can be done by hand as well (Figure 6.5). A feeler gauge and leak light allow you to make sure pads are seating properly.

Figure 6.4. Adjust Upper Bridge Key
Down (Clarinet)

Figure 6.5. Bend Upper Bridge Key
Up (Clarinet)

Woodwind
Clarinet

Common Adjustment Problems

Side B-flat Trill Key

If a clarinet does not sound more than one or two tones, the trouble is probably in the keys of the upper joint. Check to see if any keys have pads missing. If this is not the case, look for a bent key, which is probably the side B-flat trill key.

A–A-flat Combination

There is an adjustment screw on top of the left hand (throat A-flat key) (Figure 6.6).

If this adjustment screw is screwed in too far, it will not allow the left hand A-flat key to seat (Figure 6.7).

Figure 6.7 Left-Hand A-flat Key Seating (Clarinet)

Figure 6.6, A–A-flat Adjustment Screw (Clarinet)

Left-Hand Lever Keys

Located on the lower joint on the left-hand side are two long lever keys, which play the middle of the staff B-natural and C-sharp as well as below the staff low E and F-sharp (Figure 6.8).

   If the action is noisy, it is probably due to the fact that the fish skin, at the point at which the ends of the two long lever keys and the ends of the horizontal key arms join, is lost or has worn out (Figure 6.9).

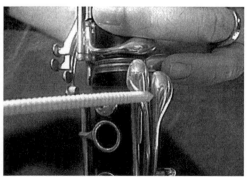

Figure 6.8. Left-Hand Lever Keys Located on Lower Joint (Clarinet)

Figure 6.9. Eliminating Noisy Action with Fish Skin Pad, Plastic Trash Bag, Plastic Food Wrap, or Teflon Tape (Clarinet)

Woodwind
Clarinet

Common Adjustment Problems

Left-Hand Lever Keys, cont.

Procedure:

1. After removing the two left-hand (vertical) lever keys, cut two small replacement squares made of about 1/4 inch from the skin of an old pad, from a plastic trash bag, or from plastic food wrap. Another suggested material is Teflon tape.

2. Dampen the squares with the tip of the tongue and place them over the holes in the end of the arms of the E–B and F-sharp–C-sharp keys. (These keys run horizontally.)

3. Dip both of the pins, located on the end of the lever keys, in key oil, and push them into place in the holes of the E–B and F-sharp–C-sharp keys.

4. Replace the left-hand lever key rods.

Additional Troubleshooting Options

Problem: Stuck tenons

Solution: When a clarinet is left together for an extended period of time, more often than not the barrel will be stuck to the top of the upper joint. The safest way to remove the stuck sections is to put them in some place cool or cold. This will shrink everything. When you remove them from the cold area, put your warm hand on the barrel, expanding it and allowing removal. (Professional repair technicians use their best judgment on amount of time left in the cool/cold.)

An alternative, but not preferred, method of removing the stuck sections is to use a sharp knife blade and insert it into the crack between the two pieces. Gently twist the knife blade enough to break the seal around the entire edge. Make sure to regrease the cork once separated by hand.

Woodwind
Clarinet

Additional Troubleshooting Options

Problem: Plays stuffy throughout

Solution: Option 1 = Check reed condition, reed placement, and ligature placement.

Option 2 = Check for leaks.

Option 3 = Check that there are no stuck swabs in the bore.

Option 4 = Try a different mouthpiece, perhaps a "step-up" brand.

Additional Troubleshooting Options

Problem: Fuzzy tone while playing (left-hand thumb)/leaks

Solution: 1. Close the pad under the throat A key of upper joint (Figure 6.10).

2. Use more cork on the underside of the arm of the key that is under the throat A key (Figure 6.11).

Figure 6.10. Close Pad under Upper Joint
– Throat A Key (Clarinet)

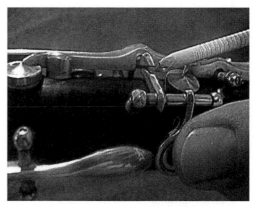

Figure 6.11. Adding Cork to Underside of
the Arm under A Key (Clarinet)

Woodwind
Clarinet

Bell Attachment

When attaching the bell to the body of the alto or bass clarinet, make sure that the body bridge key goes under the spatula of the bell key (Figure 6.12).

Figure 6.12. Proper Bell Attachment
(Bass Clarinet)

Body bridge key under the spatula of bell key

Bass Clarinet Leak

Problem: Leak (first finger left-hand F-sharp not closing enough)

Solution: The spring under the throat A key could be broken off, so look to see if part of the spring has slipped down, which could be partially blocking the key that is directly under the A key, preventing it from closing all the way.

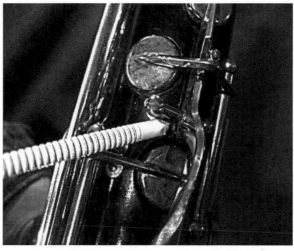

Figure 6.13. Broken Spring under Upper Joint A Key

Woodwind Clarinet

Take the A key off and replace the spring that was underneath, giving the key its tension. There is no need to take off the side A-flat key. Be careful not to lose the small screw (Figure 6.13).

Testing and Adjusting for Leaks

Oboes are very touchy. A certified repair technician should service an oboe if you are not completely comfortable making necessary adjustments.

Procedure:

1. Press down R1 with the thumb.

    - With the index finger of your right hand, press L2. Notice that L-a is lowered with this action.

    - Insert the feeler gauge under L-a, press L2, and withdraw the gauge, hopefully with an even drag. If the drag is uneven, the key (L-a) is not seating. Locate the small adjustment screw that controls this key, and turn it about one-quarter (clockwise) turn.

    - With the feeler gauge, check to see if key L2 is seating. If not, the adjustment screw for L-a has been turned too far and should be backed off slightly.

    - Continue checking until both keys are seating.

Woodwind
Oboe

2. Repeat the entire procedure with L3 and L-b.

3. Check to see if keys L-a and L-b seat when R1 is released.

   - Insert the feeler gauge under L-a then L-b, and withdraw it as you press R1 and release.
   - If there is a lack of drag, a bridge key adjustment can be made (either up or down).

4. Press and hold down L4 (G-sharp/A-flat).

   - Place the feeler gauge under the pad that comes up when L4 is pressed (G-sharp/A-flat).
   - Press R1, which should also depress the raised L4 (G-sharp/A-flat).
   - Withdraw the feeler gauge and check for drag.
   - If there is little drag, correct with the small adjustment screw or bend the key bar involved up or down.
   - Check with the gauge to make sure there has not been too much of an adjustment.
   - Check that both the L4 (G-sharp/A-flat) key and R1 are seating.

5. Insert the feeler gauge under R-a, press the R2 key, and check for drag. If there is no drag, locate the small adjustment screw between these two keys and correct as before. Insert the gauge under R2, press, and check for drag. If there is no drag, the adjustment screw that regulates R2 and R-a has been turned too far, so back it off a little. Both (R2 and R-a keys) should seat together.

6. Some oboes have an F resonator key, which is located near and connected to R3. Place the feeler gauge under this resonator key, press R3, and check the seating. If there is little or no drag, locate the small adjustment screw that controls this key; regulate and recheck until an even drag results between the resonator key and R3.

Woodwind
Oboe

7. Press L5 (low B-flat key). This also presses two padded keys (X and Y) over their tone holes.

   - Repeat this action while using the feeler gauge under one and then the other (X and Y). Look to see if either key is not sealing.

   - The adjustment for this is made by bending (up or down) the bridge key that connects the key mechanism of the lower joint to the B-flat key on the bell (Figure 7.1). (*See Practical Band Instrument Repair Manual* by Clayton H. Tiede, pp. 71–72.)

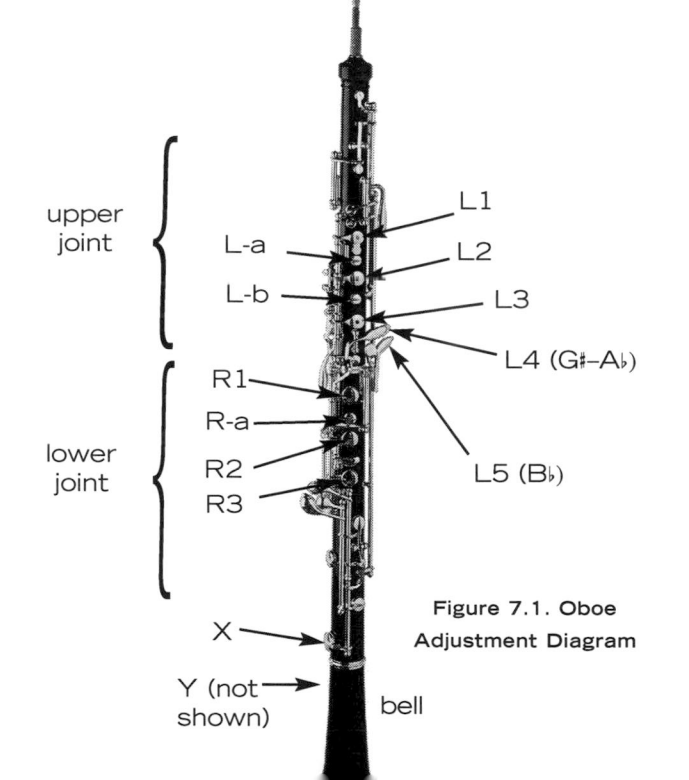

upper joint

L-a
L-b

L1
L2
L3
L4 (G♯–A♭)

lower joint

R1
R-a
R2
R3

L5 (B♭)

Figure 7.1. Oboe Adjustment Diagram

X

Y (not shown)

bell

Additional Troubleshooting Options

Problem: **A and G are stuffy**

Solution: One possible solution is to reglue the loose pad above the left-hand first finger. (Check with feeler gauge and leak light.)

Problem: **A-flat sound is garbled/stuffy**

Solution: One possible solution is to look for a pad falling away from a cup and reglue (check with feeler gauge).

Problem: **Poor or no sound**

Solution: Make sure that there are no stuck swabs in the bore.

Woodwind
Oboe

Saxophone
The Key Mechanism

Testing for Leaks

If an instrument fails to blow or plays hard, first check the reed and ligature placement. If those are fine, the trouble is usually a leak or a bent key. Leaks can be caused by poorly installed pads (often from the factory) or a tear in a pad skin.

One thing a player can do to detect a possible leak is to play starting on B-natural (in the middle of the staff). If this tone cannot be played, the leak is above this in the left-hand palm keys. If the B-natural sounds, work your way down using a feeler gauge. A "leak light" is a great way to detect leaks. Drop the leak light into the bore of the instrument, pausing under each key to be inspected.

Sticky Pads

Saliva naturally sticks to the G-sharp and E-flat keys because the keys are closed. Using a new, crisp dollar bill or a piece of paper, place the edge of the bill between the tone hole rim and the pad. Press down on the pad and slide the bill out. (Repeat this several times.)

Springs

Tension can be added to a spring if it continues to fall off the post on a key. Add tension to the spring by carefully bending it back the opposite way a little bit; straightening will lessen the tension.

The Neckpiece

Care and Emergency Repair

The mouthpiece should never be left on the neck when the instrument is put away. This causes the cork to become wobbly and leak.

For a temporarily tighter fit between the mouthpiece and the neckpiece cork, try greasing the tenon and rotating it over a flame. Keep the cork moving so it will not burn. This will temporarily cause the cork to swell. Another emergency repair for the neck tenon cork is to wrap the cork with a piece of scrap paper before putting the mouthpiece over it.

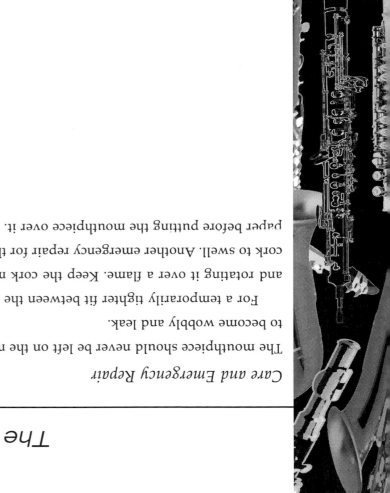

Common Adjustment Problems

Octave Mechanism

If the instrument fails to sound any notes in the low register and only those in the high register, the octave mechanism needs adjusting.

To check the adjustment, play A and G above the staff. When G is played, the octave key on the neck should be down (closed). When A is played, the octave key should be up (open).

When the octave ring is bent, the octave key on the neckpiece will be held open all the time. To ensure that the octave key will operate correctly, bend the ring back in place while holding the pad cup down (Figure 8.1).

Hold the pad cup down while pushing the octave ring in slightly.

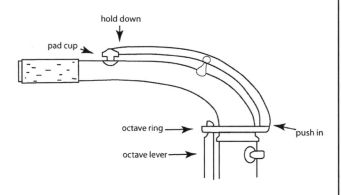

Figure 8.1. Neck: Octave Mechanism Adjustment (Saxophone)

Woodwind
Saxophone

Common Adjustment Problems

G-sharp Key

If the G-sharp pad is not opening, one reason could be that the G-sharp key spring is out of place. Simply reset it onto the post (Figure 8.2).

If the pad still does not operate, lift the pad up with your fingers. Then use a new, crisp dollar bill or a piece of paper, and insert it under the G-sharp pad and over the tone hole. Pull out the paper several times. (This helps to remove residue that has collected.)

Figure 8.2. Reset Spring onto Post Controlling G-sharp Key (Saxophone)

Problem: Leaks on D (middle of the staff)

Solution: Check for pads not closing. Loosen the adjustment screw above the first finger of the right-hand F key. Look for a possible worn pad, and replace it if needed. Check for leaks with a feeler gauge, and test for drag or use a leak light.

Problem: G-natural leaks

Solution: Visual inspection could show a leak. Press your third finger of your left hand down. This could reveal a missing pad.

Problem: Low register not speaking/wobble (wa-wa-wa-wa) sound

Solution: Look for low B-flat not sealing. This could have been bumped off of the tone hole. If so, bend it back and center it over the tone hole. Check for leaks with the feeler gauge and test for drag, or use the leak light.

Woodwind
Saxophone

Problem: Octave key slow response resulting in unwanted lost motion

Solution: To fix lost motion, try adding a rubber sleeve on the octave-key lever so there is a tiny space between the rubber sleeve and the octave ring (Figure 8.3).

Figure 8.3. Replace Missing Octave Key Rubber Sleeve (Saxophone)

Problem: **G-sharp key leaks**

Solution: The arm that sticks out, off of the G-sharp key, needs more felt (or Valentino cork) on it to force the key down to seal. Check for leaks with feeler gauge or leak light, and test for drag (Figure 8.4).

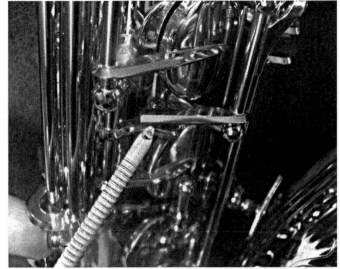

Figure 8.4. G-sharp Key Arm – Adding More Felt for Seal (Saxophone)

Woodwind
Saxophone

Additional Troubleshooting Options

Problem: G-sharp key not opening enough and sluggish

Solution: Notice the long spring that comes off the post by your left-hand middle finger G key. This spring runs down past the pinky G-sharp key arm. There is a slotted groove in the arm that lies below the G-sharp key that the long spring should rest in. (Use a spring hook to reach in and move it into position—Figure 8.5).

Figure 8.5. Replacing Long Spring behind G-sharp Key Arm (Saxophone)

Problem: E-flat key sticks on roller of low C key

Solution: Bend E-flat key up so it does not hit the roller of the C key (Figure 8.6). If the E-flat key has been forced up against the low-C key, this can be bent away by hand.

Figure 8.6. Bend E-flat Key Up (Saxophone)

The rollers of the E-flat and C keys should be at a somewhat level position with each other.

Woodwind
Saxophone

Additional Troubleshooting Options

Problem: Low C-sharp key leaks due to bent key pad

Solution: Bend key to center over tone hole (by hand). Check for leaks with feeler gauge and test for drag, or use leak light (Figure 8.7).

Figure 8.7. Bend C-sharp Key over Tone Hole (Saxophone)

Problem: Low C key leaks due to bent key pad

Solution: Bend key by hand to center it over the tone hole. Check for leaks with the feeler gauge and test for drag, or use a leak light (Figure 8.8).

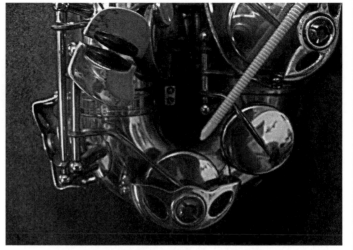

Figure 8.8. Bend C Key over Tone Hole
(Saxophone)

Woodwind
Saxophone

Additional Troubleshooting Options

Problem: Low E-flat key leaks

Solution 1: If the key guard is bent, bend the low-E-flat key guard to see if it allows the key to seal (Figure 8.9).

Solution 2: Check to see if the pad needs replacing.

Solution 3: Bend the key to center it over the tone hole. Check for leaks with a feeler gauge, or use a leak light. Test for drag.

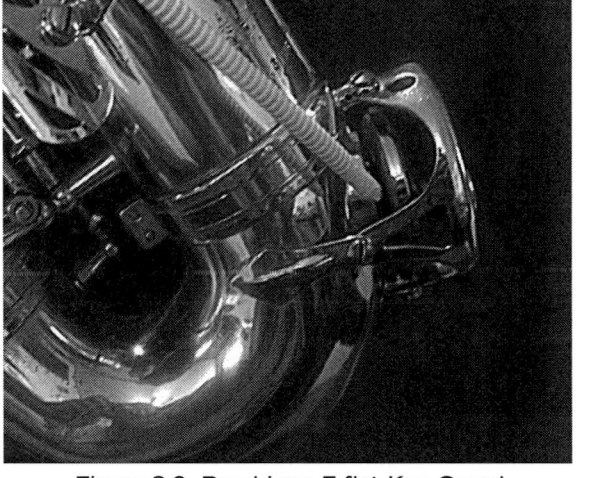

Figure 8.9. Bend Low E-flat Key Guard away from Pad (Saxophone)

Problem: **Stuffy D (middle of the staff)**

Solution: The small pad that opens up when playing D may be loose and not opening up enough. This is attached below the octave-key lever, near where the neck is inserted into the saxophone (Figure 8.10). If needed, carefully bend the octave lever back up to straight position. Use needle-nose pliers, and put a rubber cushion between the jaws of the pliers so it does not get scratched.

Figure 8.10. Stuffy D (Saxophone)

Pointing to pad that opens when playing D

Woodwind
Saxophone

Stuffy D, cont.

Bend octave lever up from the bottom on the horizontal piece where the screw is (Figure 8.11). A stuffy D could also be caused by the low-C key being too close to the tone hole or the low-C key guard being bent.

Figure 8.11. Bend Octave Lever to Straighten Position (Saxophone)

Problem: B key (middle of the staff) not sealing

Solution: Put the felt strip under the arm under the B key, or use the adjustment screw (Figure 8.12).

Figure 8.12. Felt Strip Needed under B Key Arm or Use Adjustment Screw (Saxophone)

Woodwind
Saxophone

91

Problem: Lost motion on low C-sharp key

Solution: Replace the rubber sleeve, or add a felt strip on end of the C-sharp key arm (Figure 8.13).

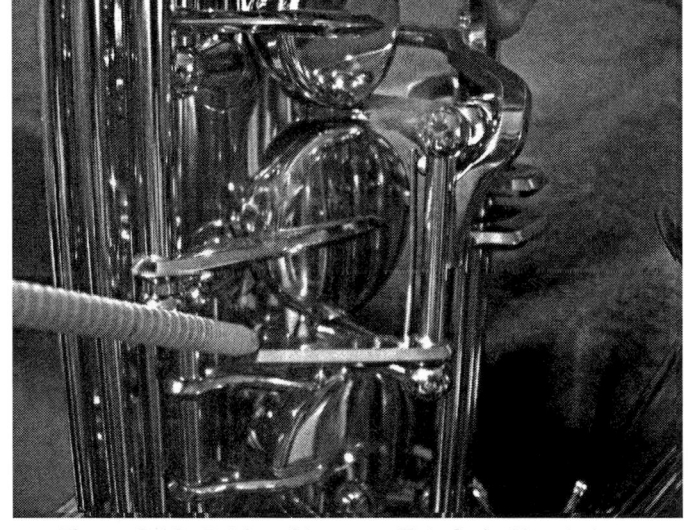

Figure 8.13. Rubber Sleeve or Felt Strip Needed on End of C-sharp Key Arm (Saxophone)

Problem: Low B-flat key (left-hand pinky key) is opening too far and not sealing

Solution: Put additional Valentino cork or felt on the front side of the arm that is connected to the low B-natural pedal key (left-hand pinky). Thus, the back side of the low B-flat pedal key will butt up against the Valentino cork or felt that was glued to the low-B pedal key (Figure 8.14).

Figure 8.14. Valentino Cork Attached to Low B-natural Pedal Key Arm (Saxophone)

This butts up against the back of the low B-flat pedal key.

Woodwind
Saxophone

Additional Troubleshooting Options

Problem: F-sharp not speaking

When the F-sharp key is depressed, this should result in the key pad that is above the first finger (on the right hand) closing all of the way.

Solution: Locate the long rod on the opposite side of the saxophone (directly across from the right-hand keys). This rod is under a guard. This key rod has two arms attached to a parallel rod. These arms need enough cork (Figure 8.15) to allow the key pad above the right-hand first finger to seal when the middle F-sharp key is depressed.

Figure 8.15. F-sharp Not Speaking (Saxophone)

Check for enough cork under the two arms coming off of the long rod that controls the F and F-sharp keys (under the guard), to allow the key pad that is above the right-hand first finger to seal when the middle F-sharp key is depressed.

Woodwind
Saxophone

Flute
The Key Mechanism

Testing and Adjusting for Leaks

When a flute player has difficulty playing low notes, there is probably a leaking pad. Make sure that all springs up and down the flute are connected to the posts. Using a crochet or spring hook works well.

When trying to use the adjustment screws to reseat pads that are not sealing, be careful to not turn the screws too far either way because the adjustment screws control the seating of more than one pad at a time.

Additional Troubleshooting Options

Problem: Airy sound

Solution: Possibly use the adjustment screw (right-hand first finger).

Problem: Low-C key not sealing

Solution: Put thin Valentino cork as a shim under the roller key.

Problem: Gemeinhardt/pads not sealing (especially F-sharp)

Solution: Start with the adjustment screw on the right-hand third finger F-sharp. Tighten it so that the pad just above the right-hand first finger F seals. Then adjust other screws, but not too much. Watch that all pads are sealing and others are staying closed during adjustments.

Problem: Armstrong/low F-sharp key too high

Solution: Look to see if the cork under the arm behind the F-sharp key is missing. If so, replace it with Valentino cork (sized to fit).

Problem: Armstrong/G-natural not speaking

Solution: Notice that the key above the right-hand first finger has a small key that extends over it. This small key should not be touching the larger key under it. The key may have been bumped and, as a result, is now bent. Carefully bend it back up to a level position over the larger key.

Woodwind
Flute

Additional Troubleshooting Options

Problem: Gemeinhardt/loose adjustment screw (first finger, right hand) resulting in pad above right-hand first finger leaking

Solution: Take clear nail polish and coat the threads of the screw. Add a strand of hair, carefully wrap it around the threads, and insert the screw back into the hole.

Problem: Gemeinhardt/stuffy middle of the staff D

Solution: Check to see if the foot joint E-flat key is sealing. Check the condition of the E-flat pad. If the pad is hitting the pad cup more on one side than the other, you might try taking the E-flat key off. Then bend the pad cup up so that it is in an L position in relationship to the E-flat key. Be careful not to bend it too much.

Additional Troubleshooting Options

Problem: Armstrong/A-flat key not sealing

Solution: The goal is to take the A-flat key off and carefully bend it into an L shape in relationship to the A-flat key arm. First, take off the keys surrounding the screw that holds the A-flat key in place. Give the A-flat spring a little extra tension once you have the room to reach it. Carefully bending the spring in the opposite direction should provide the extra tension needed to force the A-flat key down for a tighter seal. Remember to lay the keys or rods out in such a way that you will remember how you removed them.

Additional Troubleshooting Options

Problem: Poor or no sound

Solution: Make sure that there are no stuck swabs of any sort in the body of the flute.

Problem: Loose head joint cork and crown

Solution: Pull out the head joint, and screw down the top washer on the tuning cork, causing the cork to bulge. Another method is to coat the cork with cork grease and heat it up with a lighter. The cork will swell. Insert it from the bottom of the head joint and reposition with the crown on top. Use the cleaning rod and notch to center the cork in relation to the center of the lip plate.

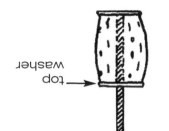

top washer

Figure 9.1. Exposed Head Joint Cork (Flute)

Problem: Armstrong/key below
A-flat key is stuck

Solution: Long rods run the length of the body. As you follow the long rods to the bottom end of the body, notice that the longest rod that is closest to the foot joint (E-flat key) has a small screw in the end (Figure 9.1). This screw is in the end of the longest rod, nearest to the E-flat key of the foot joint, and it is too tight and binding within the rod. Thus, loosen the screw very slightly until the A-flat key pad is loose enough to move freely.

Figure 9.2. Key Below A-flat Key Is Stuck (Flute)

Loosen the screw in the end of the longest rod and closest to the foot joint E-flat key

Woodwind
Flute

Chapter 10
Summary

Final Thoughts

Almost daily, students approach the director with band instruments in need of repair. Sometimes the students ask to make a repair during a band lesson or in the middle of rehearsals.

Being comfortable with minor or emergency repairs will save valuable lesson or rehearsal time and money on unnecessary repairs. Neglect or the wrong Band-aid remedy can cause minor repairs to eat away at the band budget and create instrument shortages.

Instruments will give years of service if a small amount of time is spent on routine care. It is very important that proper cleaning and maintenance procedures be carried out on a regular basis.

More time can be devoted to teaching music, not fixing instruments, if you insist on students playing high-quality instruments, not "throw away" discount store specials. Next, teach your students how to respect and maintain their instruments. Finally, develop a professional working relationship with a certified repair technician and competent music store. They will support your program and help you stretch your budget and your time.

APPENDIX

Trumpet/Cornet

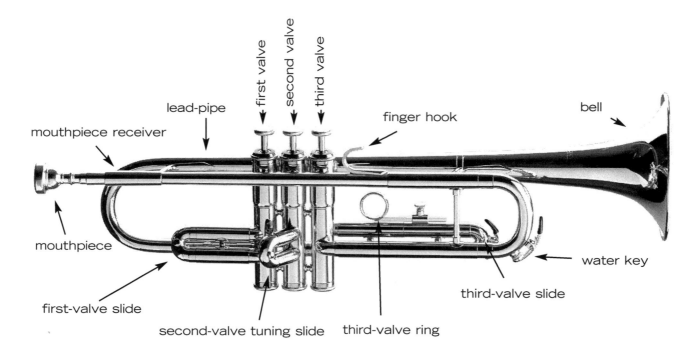

first valve

second valve

third valve

lead-pipe

finger hook

bell

mouthpiece receiver

mouthpiece

water key

first-valve slide

third-valve slide

second-valve tuning slide

third-valve ring

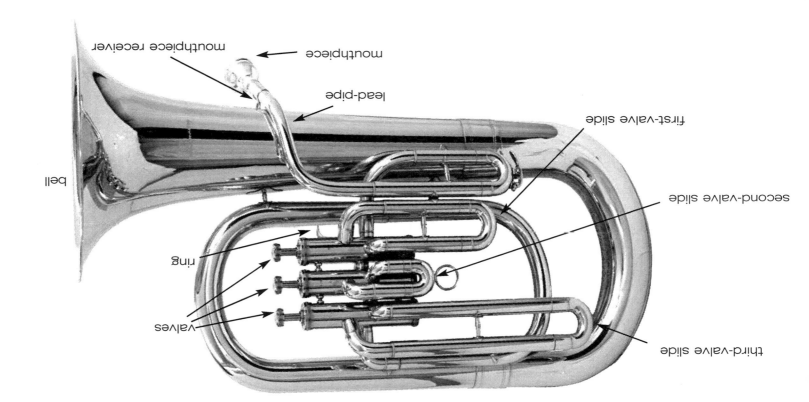

mouthpiece receiver

mouthpiece

lead-pipe

first-valve slide

second-valve slide

bell

ring

third-valve slide

valves

Euphonium

Baritone vs. Euphonium

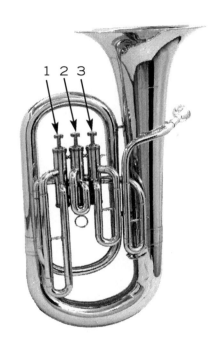

Baritone

Euphonium

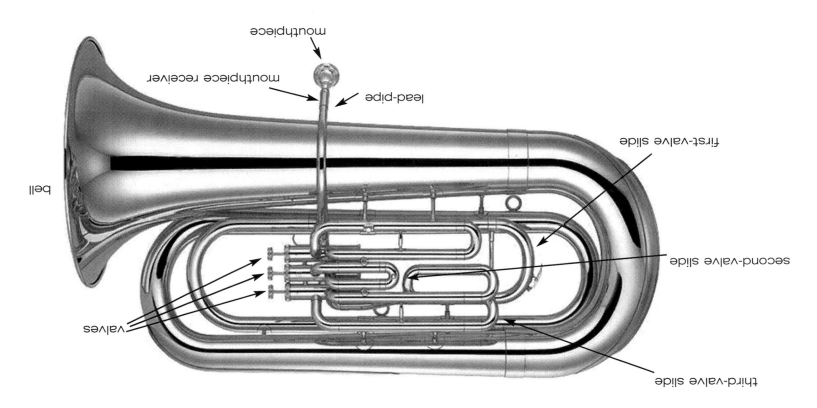

mouthpiece

mouthpiece receiver

lead-pipe

bell

first-valve slide

second-valve slide

valves

third-valve slide

Tuba

Trombone

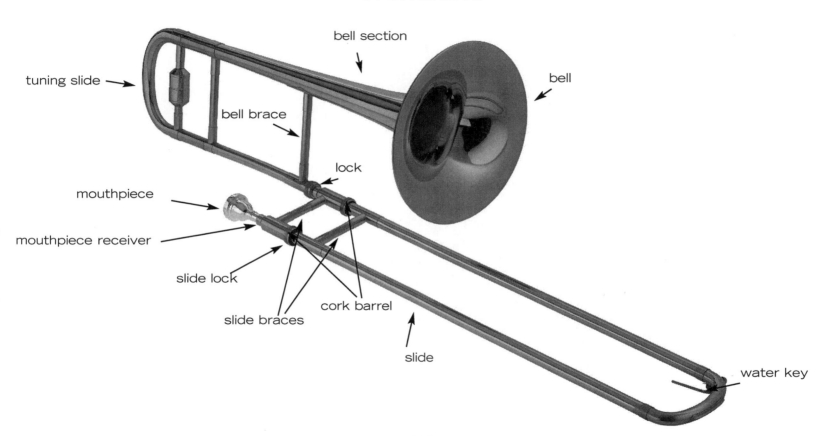

tuning slide

bell section

bell

bell brace

lock

mouthpiece

mouthpiece receiver

slide lock

slide braces

cork barrel

slide

water key

mouthpiece

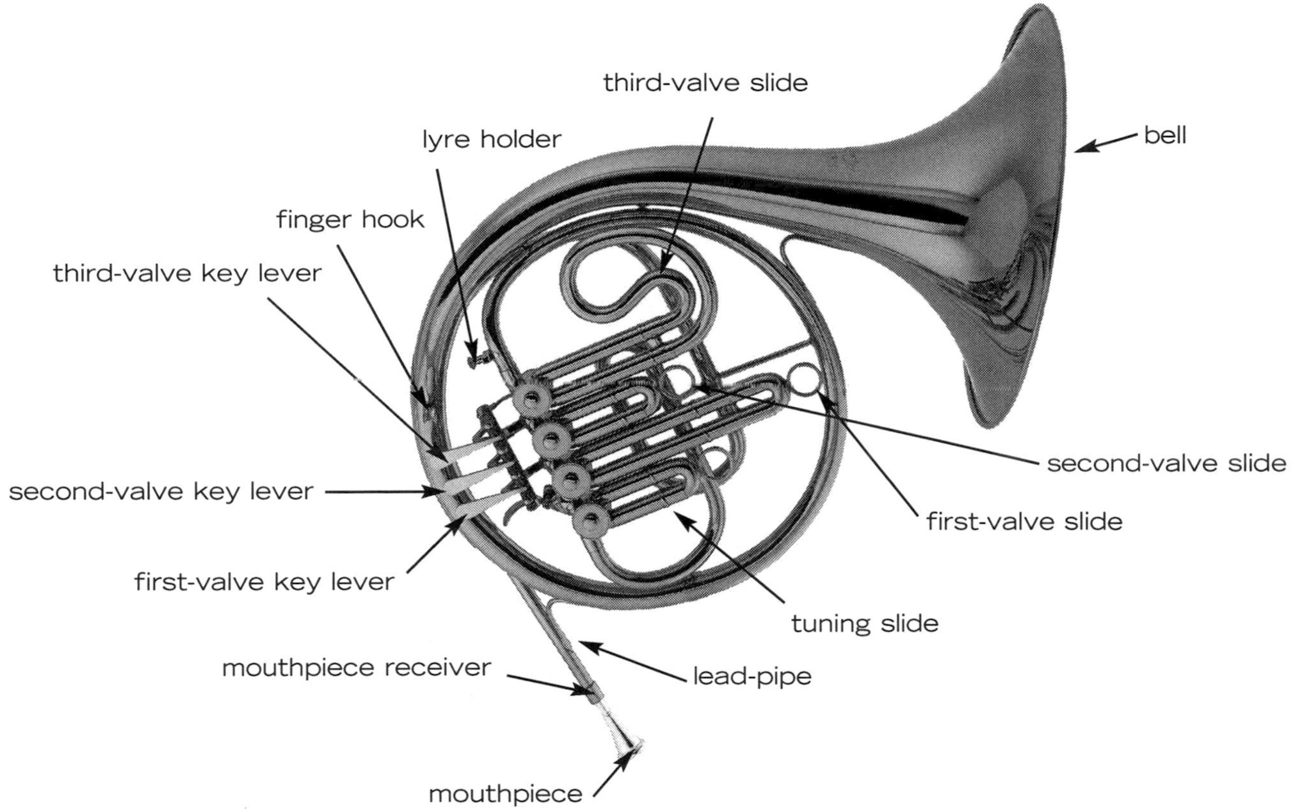

mouthpiece receiver

lead-pipe

tuning slide

first-valve key lever

first-valve slide

second-valve key lever

second-valve slide

third-valve key lever

finger hook

bell

lyre holder

third-valve slide

French Horn

Clarinet

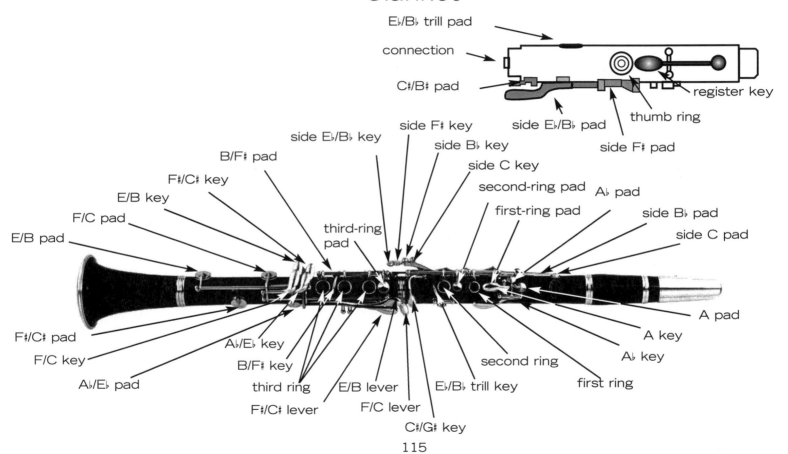

E♭/B♭ trill pad

connection

C♯/B♯ pad

side F♯ key

side E♭/B♭ key

side B♭ key

side C key

side E♭/B♭ pad

thumb ring

register key

side F♯ pad

second-ring pad

A♭ pad

first-ring pad

side B♭ pad

side C pad

B/F♯ pad

F♯/C♯ key

E/B key

F/C pad

E/B pad

third-ring pad

A pad

A key

F♯/C♯ pad

F/C key

A♭/E♭ pad

A♭/E♭ key

B/F♯ key

third ring

F♯/C♯ lever

E/B lever

F/C lever

C♯/G♯ key

E♭/B♭ trill key

second ring

first ring

A♭ key

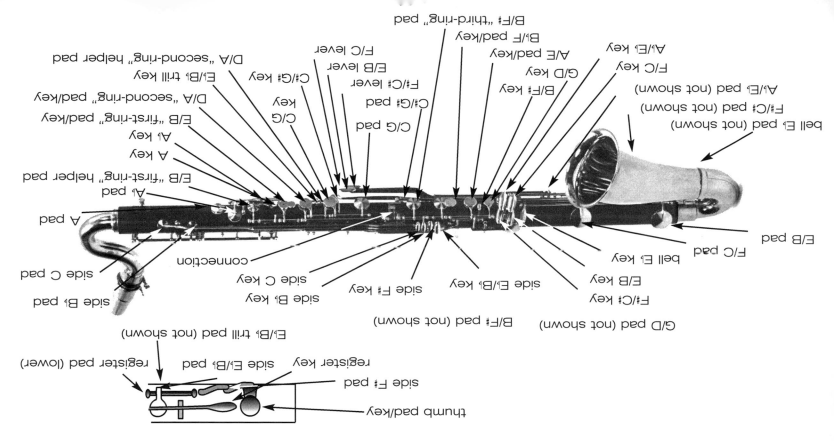

Bass Clarinet

A♭ "second-ring" helper pad
D/A "second-ring" pad/key
E♭/B♭ trill key
A♭ "second-ring" pad/key
E/B "first-ring" pad/key
A♭ key
A key
E/B "first-ring" helper pad
A♭ pad
A pad
side C pad
side B♭ pad
E♭/B♭ trill pad (not shown)
register pad (lower)
register key
side E♭/B♭ pad
side F♯ pad
thumb pad/key

connection
side B♭ key
side C key
side F♯ key
B/F♯ pad (not shown)
side E♭/B♭ key
E/B key
G/D pad (not shown)

C/G key
C/G pad
C♯/G♯ key
C♯/G♯ pad
F♯/C♯ lever
E♯/B lever
F/C lever
B♯/F♯ pad
B/F♯ key
A/E pad/key
G/D key
B/F♯ "third-ring" pad
B♯/F♯ pad/key
A♭/E♭ key
F/C key
A♭/E♭ pad (not shown)
F♯/C♯ pad (not shown)
bell E♭ pad (not shown)

E/B pad
F/C pad
bell E♭ key
F♯/C♯ key

Oboe

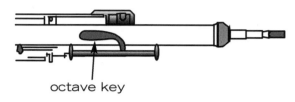

octave key

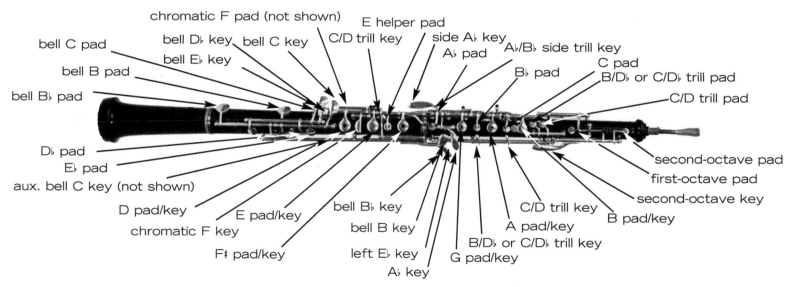

chromatic F pad (not shown)

E helper pad

bell C pad

bell D♭ key   bell C key

C/D trill key

side A♭ key

A♭/B♭ side trill key

bell E♭ key

A♭ pad

C pad

bell B pad

B♭ pad

B/D♭ or C/D♭ trill pad

bell B♭ pad

C/D trill pad

D♭ pad

E♭ pad

aux. bell C key (not shown)

second-octave pad

first-octave pad

D pad/key

second-octave key

chromatic F key

E pad/key

bell B♭ key

C/D trill key

B pad/key

A pad/key

F♯ pad/key

bell B key

B/D♭ or C/D♭ trill key

left E♭ key

G pad/key

A♭ key

117

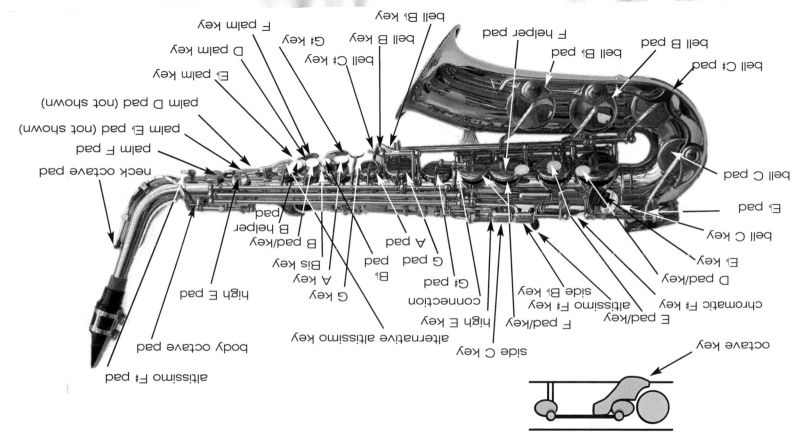

Saxophone

Flute

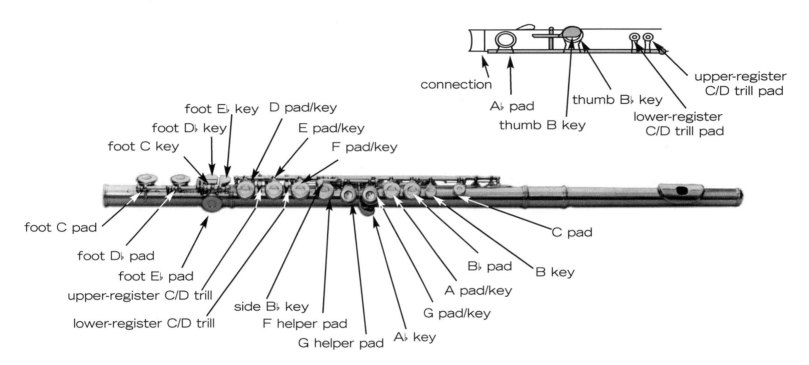

connection

A♭ pad

thumb B key

thumb B♭ key

upper-register
C/D trill pad

lower-register
C/D trill pad

foot E♭ key

foot D♭ key

foot C key

D pad/key

E pad/key

F pad/key

foot C pad

C pad

foot D♭ pad

foot E♭ pad

B♭ pad

B key

upper-register C/D trill

A pad/key

lower-register C/D trill

side B♭ key

F helper pad

G helper pad

A♭ key

G pad/key

Acknowledgments

Dawn Biba: Technical assistance

Maribeth Biba: Piano consultant and band accessories, Heid Music

Nick Keelan: Lawrence University Conservatory of Music, Appleton, Wisconsin

Trea Kimball: Print music and instrument sales, Heid Music

Ron Polum: Repair shop service manager, Heid Music

Lynda Sullivan: Saint Mary's University, Minneapolis, Minnesota

About the Author

Gregory Biba has had first-hand experience with emergency band instrument repair and maintenance for many years as a K–12 band director. He is now director of bands in the Waupaca (Wisconsin) Public Schools.

He received his bachelor degree in music education from Lawrence University in Appleton, Wisconsin, and his master of music education from St. Mary's University of Minnesota.

Biba is an active member of the Wisconsin School Music Association and the Music Educators National Conference, as well as the Inventors Network of Wisconsin. Throughout his career, he has recognized the importance of saving time and money around the classroom. Several of his inventions have been patented.